God's

BITS AND PIECES

Thank you for all of your prayers & support. I pray that God blesses you as you read through these devotions.

Love & prayers

Stephanie Padgett Widener

9/18/2022

God's

Bits and Pieces

A devotional with purpose

Stephanie P. Widener

XULON PRESS ELITE

Xulon Press Elite
2301 Lucien Way #415
Maitland, FL 32751
407.339.4217
www.xulonpress.com

Unless otherwise indicated, Scripture quotations taken from the King James Version (KJV)–*public domain.*

Scripture quotations taken from the New King James Version (NKJV). Copyright © 1982 by Thomas Nelson, Inc. Used by permission. All rights reserved.

Scripture quotations taken from the English Standard Version (ESV). Copyright © 2001 by Crossway, a publishing ministry of Good News Publishers. Used by permission. All rights reserved.

Scripture quotations taken from the Holy Bible, New Living Translation (NLT). Copyright ©1996, 2004, 2007 by Tyndale House Foundation. Used by permission of Tyndale House Publishers, Inc.

Scripture quotations taken from the Holy Bible, New International Version (NIV). Copyright © 1973, 1978, 1984, 2011 by Biblica, Inc.™. Used by permission. All rights reserved.

Scripture quotations taken from the Amplified Bible (AMP). Copyright © 1954, 1958, 1962, 1964, 1965, 1987 by The Lockman Foundation. Used by permission. All rights reserved.

Paperback ISBN-13: 978-1-6628-1669-7
Hard Cover ISBN-13: 978-1-6628-1670-3
Ebook ISBN-13: 978-1-6628-1671-0

Just a quick thought for today...

- -

Pursing Happiness

So many times, we try to look for happiness in the things of this world, like jobs, homes, cars, money, friends and so on; but the only true happiness is found in Jesus Christ. The Bible tells us in Matthew 6:33 (KJV), "But seek ye first the kingdom of God, and his righteousness; and all these things shall be added unto you."

When you seek God and put Him first, He will add the other things that make you happy. He knows that your heart desires materialistic items, but you cannot put materialistic things before Him. When your desires take priority before the true and living God and you begin seeking those things to fulfill your happiness, they become your god. The Bible tells us in Psalms 37:4 (NIV), "Take delight in the LORD, and he will give you the desires of your heart."

God wants what is best for you and He wants to fulfill the desires of your heart, but first you must seek Him. Never stop seeking Him. He will fulfill your happiness.

Be blessed.

Just a quick thought for today...

- -

God is faith full

Lord I don't know what you're up to today, but I know you're working on my behalf and great things are coming our way. I declare it in the name of Jesus! Nothing the enemy has planned will prosper. Today is a new season in my life and by faith I trust and believe my year of jubilee has come. I may not see it, but by faith I declare and receive it.

If you trust that God is a great God, and can provide just what you need then I challenge you to start declaring it today!

Psalms 89:5 (NLT), "All heaven will praise your great wonders, LORD; myriads of angels will praise you for your faithfulness." Together let's flood heaven with praise for the God we serve is a mighty miracle working God!!

Be blessed.

Just a quick thought for today...

- -

Wait on the Lord

When you are praying for a particular request, sometimes God makes you wait to gain valuable insight. Psalms 27:14 (NASB), "Wait for the LORD; Be strong and let your heart take courage; Yes, wait for the LORD."

He's not making you wait to punish you. That's not who He is. He is a loving and gracious God who wants the very best for His children and sometimes what we are praying for, might not be what is best for us at that moment. His plans for your life are so much higher than your plans. So, you have to learn to trust that He truly knows best and walk by faith and not by sight. It's hard to do, but if you love God, you must follow His plan and trust it's for your good!

Be blessed.

Just a quick thought for today...

- -

Enjoy life

Make the most of every day. Take time to enjoy life. Learn to laugh and smile! Sometimes we allow the situations or circumstances around us dictate our way, but you have to learn that through each trial God is teaching life lessons. Remember it won't rain always, the sun will shine again and you will be stronger because of your trial.

Begin each day with prayer asking God what does He have for you to learn today? When you face each day with God, He has a way of making things seem brighter, no matter the circumstance you may be facing.

Philippians 4:6-7 (KJV), "Be careful for nothing; but in everything by prayer and supplication with thanksgiving let your requests be made known unto God. And the peace of God, which passeth all understanding, shall keep your hearts and minds through Christ Jesus."

Be blessed.

Just a quick thought for today...

- -

Victory

No matter what you are facing whether good or bad, know that it did not catch God off guard. You can choose to worry about it or praise Him. He's going to receive the glory for the outcome anyway, so start praising your way to victory!

Acts 16:25 (KJV), "But at midnight Paul and Silas were praying and singing hymns to God, and the prisoners were listening to them."

Be blessed.

We win

The more you stand for Jesus, the harder the devil fights against you. You have to be strong on the battlefield and guard your mind, your heart, your soul, your body, your family and your beliefs. The enemy is out to destroy whoever gets in his way of defeating God's people and as Christians you have to be on guard day and night. Understand that when he's attacking you, that it means your victory is just ahead and he's going to do everything he can to stop your victory march!

Declare this today: I choose today to march forward toward my victory and press toward the goal that God has set before me. I may face trials and battles along the way and be weary from the fight, but I will never give up! I've come too far to turn back now and I know my victory is just ahead!! So today rather than walk in defeat, I will hold my head up and declare my victory march and put the devil where he belongs—-under my feet!! I am made victorious through Jesus Christ and I've read the back of the book and I WIN!!!

Don't give up just when you're on the brink of your miracle. Remember God has this even when you don't see it!!

Galatians 6:9 (NKJV), "And let us not grow weary while doing good, for in due season we shall reap if we do not lose heart."

Be blessed.

Just a quick thought for today...

- -

Suspicious minds

With everything that is going on in today's world, be mindful to not let your naturally suspicious minds be fueled by the negative thoughts or behavior of those around you, but instead learn to love those that seek to cause you hurt. For example, if someone at church told you what another person said or thought of you; instead of allowing Satan to fuel negativity and plant seeds of anger and hate, approach the person with love. What you don't want is for that person to sit in front of you in church and while they are worshiping, you begin thinking of them as a hypocrite because your feelings toward this individual are now sour and fueled by anger, placed there by second hand information. Before you know it, Satan has you so blinded, bound and boiling with anger to the point where you can't worship and you miss your blessing

The Bible tells us in Matthew 5:23-24, that if we have an issue with someone we are to go to that person and make it right before we bring our gifts to the altar. In other words, you are just as wrong as they are by harboring ill feelings toward them. Don't let the lies of the enemy keep you bound. Make it right. Go to that person ask them to forgive you if you have offended them in anyway. You might be surprised to learn they never even said it or had any ill thoughts towards you.

By turning one another against each other, Satan can tear down the body of Christ and destroy us from the inside out. So, try something different today, start building your neighbor up with words of love and encouragement and start with those closes to you. You have to be the example that the world looks at because this world is so full of hate, anger and turmoil that scripture is unfolding right before our eyes. You must take a stand as a Christians and let the world see Jesus through you.

Be blessed.

- -

Guard your mind

Often, when we are going through a trial or fighting a battle, Satan likes to whisper things like, "If God loves you then He wouldn't make you go through this" or "if God truly cared for you, then this wouldn't have happened. If Satan can make you think you're not loved or that God doesn't have your best interest at heart, then he has successfully fulfilled his mission of planting seeds of unbelief, doubt and worry. When struggles, trials, and hardships come your way, and they always do, you have a choice; you can stand on God's word and cast all your cares, concerns and anxieties on Him or you can choose to fall prey to Satan's lies. Choose to stand firm on God's promises and He will see you through this time, the next time and the time after that. God never said being a Christian would be a bed of roses or a walk in the park, but He did promise that when we walked through the fire we would not be burned and that He would be with us every step of the way!

The Bible tells us in Psalms 91:1-2 (KJV), "He that dwelleth in the secret place of the Most High shall abide under the shadow of the Almighty. I will say of the Lord, He is my refuge and my fortress: my God; in him will I trust."

We have to learn to trust God no matter what we are facing, especially now during these unsettling times we are living in. We have to know without a shadow of a doubt that God has us in the palm of His hands. We may not know what tomorrow holds, but we truly know who holds tomorrow.

Be blessed.

Just a quick thought for today...

- -

God's creations

Stop for a minute and look around at God's beautiful creation. As I sit by the pool listening to the trees rustling as the wind gently blows through the leaves, I am reminded of the beauty in God's creations. He created all things; people, culture, language, countries, rivers, seas and lakes, and when He was finished, He said it was good.

We have allowed sin, hate and bitterness to blind us from what God has called good. Instead of looking at one another through the eyes of God and seeing the heart, we choose to only look at the outward appearance. When we learn to get back to our first love, Jesus Christ, then we will be able to love the heart of one another and look past the outward shell, the physical appearance that is worn, frail and scared According to Jeremiah 29:11 (NIV), "For I know the plans I have for you, declares the Lord, plans to prosper you and not to harm you, plans to give you hope and a future."

Don't let hate keep you from Gods plans. Start today and learn to love God's creation: all creation, big, small, good, bad, ugly and beautiful; after all it's written in His word in John 13:34 (NIV), "A new command I give you: Love one another. As I have loved you, so you must love one another."

Be blessed.

Grace

So, I hate to be the one to tell you, but YOU ARE NOT PERFECT, AND NEITHER AM I. There I said it. So many times, we feel like we have to be perfect to live for Christ and that's just not true. No matter how hard we try we will never be perfect. The Bible tells us, we are God's workmanship which means He's working on us daily! Thank God for His amazing grace and forgiveness that covers our imperfections. We are to strive to live a holy life, but there are times where we sin or mess up and not necessarily on purpose, but when we do, we are to ask for God's forgiveness, pick ourselves up and keep walking our Christian walk.

For example, the Bible says worrying is a sin. While we don't intentionally worry, it is embedded in us that just happens, some worry more than others, however, Romans 3:23 (KJV) "We have all sinned and come short of the glory of God. In II Corinthians Jesus says, "My grace is sufficient for you, for My strength is made perfect in weakness."

Remember that there was only one perfect person and that was Jesus and they crucified Him, but He rose on that third day that you and I, who are sinners can be saved and forgiven through the shedding of His blood. You will make mistakes, but don't dwell on them. Ask for forgiveness and move on and thank God for His grace and mercy.

Be blessed.

Just a quick thought for today...

- -

What's your purpose?

So many of us are trying to pursue what makes them happy. Whether it is a new job, a new house, graduating from high school or college, getting married, having a baby, but you need to ensure your first pursuit is chasing after God.

Have you even asked God what His purpose or plan is for your life? Where does He want to position you? If where you are now is making you miserable and unhappy, then look to God and ask Him for guidance and wisdom. Stop running from person to person trying to seek their advice on what you should be doing. Go straight to the source, the author of true happiness and ask Him. When you pursue God first, the Bible advises that He will add all the rest You have to be confident in knowing and trusting that God has your back and will never steer you wrong. If you go down the wrong path, it is not God's fault, so don't blame it on Him. Instead blame it on your own poor judgment.

So today I urge you, to seek His will for your life, before you make a decision of what you think is right. In Christ, chasing and pursing Him, is where you will find true happiness. Money isn't everything and sometimes causes more damage than good.

A simple prayer: "Lord help me to pursue You and allow me to allow You to take care of the rest."

Proverbs 3:5-6 (KJV), "Trust in the LORD with all your heart, And lean not on your own understanding; In all your ways acknowledge Him, And He shall direct your paths."

Be blessed.

Just a quick thought for today...

- -

Responsibility

As humans, adults and children alike, we need to learn to take responsibility for ourselves. We alone can control how we talk, walk, act, respond, treat and interact with one another. When we say things like, "the devil made me do it," we are giving Satan too much credit and power over our lives. Only you can control whether or not you will act on your impulsive thoughts, or be slow to anger. We, you need to pray that God will control your thoughts, speech and actions. Once you have control over your thoughts and actions, it allows you to live a better life and you learn to love more and be more tolerant of others. In Galatians 6:5 (NLT) the Bible tells us, "For we are each responsible for our own conduct."

Be blessed.

Just a quick thought for today...

- - - - - - - - - - - - - - - - - - - -

Stinking Thinking

How many of you know someone who's either always negative or always positive there is no in between? I bet somebody came to your mind immediately...we all know someone!! I'm sure you know someone who is always negative with no bone of positivity in them. As you are reading this, that person probably came to your mind immediately.

If you constantly dwell on the negative then you are allowing Satan to steal your joy, peace and blessings. Yes, there are times where you will face a situation and become discouraged and wonder, "why me Lord?" There have been quite a few times when things would go wrong and I felt like throwing my hands up and saying I quit, but my kids would say to me "mama that's not what God would want you to do we have to trust He is going to make a way," (so blessed to know I have raised my kids to trust God no matter what). Let me tell you, that is extremely hard to do when you see the situation you are faced with and have no idea what to do. But because of who I am, I quickly remember that I am a child of God and I immediately apologize and ask God to forgive me for wanting to quit and ask Him to help me see the positive that will come from this situation.

I have been praying for years for my year of jubilee, has it come to pass? Not yet. While I could be very negative and begin to doubt, I choose to stay positive and keep believing that God is going to do what he said and it will happen!

Sometimes even in your darkest hour you have to try and focus on something positive that may come out of your time of despair. Call on the name of Jesus and began to ask him to fill you with His joy, peace and laughter. He will give you joy that is unspeakable and fill you with His glory!! Choose today to dwell on the positives, not the negatives and see if your day is different—better. Give all your worries to God, He knows how to handle them better than we can, (it's so much easier said than done, I know. I'm encouraging myself through this whole message as well). Allow Him to turn your frown into a smile.

"Let the Spirit change your way of thinking."

Be blessed.

- - - - - - - - - - - - - - - - - - - -

A clear mind

How many times have you found yourself where you just needed clarity in a situation? You prayed and prayed, sought God's will, but still you just couldn't get peace about things and then you came into God's presence and everything seemed clear and okay.

At practice one night, we were singing 'In the Presence of Jehovah' and this thought came to me: if people would learn to get out of their own way and start pushing their way into God's presence what a difference this world would be.

We have become a generation of I want it my way or no way, and look where that has gotten us. The Bible tells us in Luke 9:23 (NLT), "Then he said to the crowd, "If any of you wants to be my follower, you must give up your own way, take up your cross daily, and follow me."

You have to get past wanting your way and be willing to do it God's way. You have to be willing to be placed on the potter's wheel and be molded and made into what Christ wants you to be. When we learn to submit to Christ, that tug of war within yourself becomes less and less. Start praying today that God gives you the mind to learn His ways, ears to hear His voice, eyes to see clear and a heart to love everyone.

Be blessed!

Just a quick thought for today...

- -

Unconditional love

What do the words unconditional love mean to you?

It means you love without any strings attached. You love with all of your heart, no matter what that person did or does to you. Think about how much Jesus loves you. He willingly took the weight of the whole world, their sins and your sins on His shoulders, loved you even before you were born, and died so that you may have life. He loved everyone He encountered no regard to their position or past.

Think about your loved ones; what you would do or give up for them can't even begin to compare to how much Jesus loves you. So today, I challenge you to love as Jesus loved, after all this is His commandment in John 15:12. Show someone a random act of kindness, let the world see Jesus through you.

Be blessed.

- -

How's your attitude

A negative mindset will get you nowhere. If you go around being negative all the time, others will want to stay far away from you. If that's you and you know you're a negative person, always seeing the bad in every situation, start today by asking God to change your attitude and to help you learn to follow Proverbs 3:5-6 and trust in Him. Start expecting good things to happen to you and through you. With God's help and determination, you can start to break that negative mindset and start experiencing all of God's blessings.

The devil knows if he can keep you with a negative attitude, he can keep you from experiencing God's goodness and stop you from getting your breakthrough. The Bible tells us that weeping may endure through the night, but JOY comes in the morning. Just because you are human, you will have trials and tribulations, but oh what a Savior you have that walks beside you and carries you through until you reach your victory. Start living in the positive and put the negative stinking attitude behind you. To grow with God, you can't keep being negative because He's definitely not negative.

Be blessed.

Just a quick thought for today...

- -

Redemption

The blood. Have you ever really taken a moment and thought about the blood of Jesus? It was shed freely for you and works like a cleansing agent by cleaning and protecting you from sin. When you ask Jesus to forgive you of your sins, His blood washes them away. His blood is precious before the Father and it should be precious to you. Jesus' blood was shed so that you may have eternal life with Him. We are made whole by the shedding of Jesus' blood. The blood will never lose its power. Thank God for His redeeming blood (Hebrews 9:15). For this reason, He is the mediator of a new covenant. Meaning, Jesus sacrificed His life as redemption for the transgressions that were committed under the first covenant, those who have been called may receive the promise of the eternal inheritance.

Be blessed.

- -

What's your talent?

What calling or gift has God given to you? Are you using that gift to the fullest and to bring glory to God? You have been given a calling or gift from God, whether it's preaching, teaching, singing, being an encourager, managing, baking- whatever it is, do it with your whole heart and to bring glory to God. Never take for granted what God has called you to do. He knew your calling long before you were born.

"God will make this happen, for he who calls you is faithful". Today ask God what gift he has for you and then use them to uplift him" (I Thessalonians 5: 24 NLT).

Be blessed.

Legacy

What legacy will you leave behind once this life is over?
What will they say about you?

There are no do overs once your life is complete, this is not a video game where we get multiple lives. God grants you multiple chances to get this one life right, but your days are numbered. That song "Live like you were dying," is one of the truest statements. You should live as if there are no tomorrows because the Bible tells us in James 4:14 (NLT), "Why, you do not even know what will happen tomorrow. What is your life? You are a mist that appears for a little while and then vanishes."

You need to learn to live this life with love, forgiveness and honor. Don't let this day pass without showing others the love of Christ, the mercy of forgiveness and words that bring Him honor and glory. Start truly living today, by asking Jesus to first forgive you and show you how to forgive others. Second, ask Him to help you love like He loves, without conditions or judging. Lastly, ask Him to ensure that every word, deed or action brings Him honor.

Be blessed.

Just a quick thought for today...

- - - - - - - - - - - - - - - - - - - -

Power

When the word church is mentioned, one automatically thinks of a building with four walls, a gathering place to come together to worship, maybe see friends or family, hear a couple of songs and listen to the pastor preacher. While this is true, it is only half correct. The other half to this truth is that you, are the church. You are the body of Christ, not a building.

In Acts 1:8(NLT) states, "But you will receive power when the Holy Spirit comes upon you. And you will be my witnesses, telling people about me everywhere—in Jerusalem, throughout Judea, in Samaria, and to the ends of the earth."

As being the body of Christ, you have to get out of those four walls and reach out to those around us. I was reading a post one morning about a garbage man who noticed an elderly lady had not put her trash can out for several weeks and when he checked on her, he found she had no trash because she had run out of food. He took it upon himself to help her out and bought her groceries. He was being the church by showing kindness.

When was the last time you showed a random act of kindness? The article went on to say the church could be a phone call to just check on someone, a card to let them know you miss them, a bag of groceries for someone who's down on their luck, or a monetary gift to help pay a bill when they're a little short. Jesus tells us in 1 Peter 4:10 (NLT), "God has given each of you a gift from his great variety of spiritual gifts. Use them well to serve one another."

We can be the church anywhere and anytime. God is with us all the time. Let's not confine Him to a building, but spread His gospel to others outside of that building so others may come to know his goodness, mercy and grace.

It's time for the church to make a move and step out of our comfort zone to show this world the true meaning of loving one another just as Christ has loved the church.

Be blessed.

- -

Hope

What are you believing for? Do you have enough faith to believe that your prayers are going to be answered? Hebrews 11:1 (NLT), "Faith shows the reality of what we hope for; it is the evidence of things we cannot see."

You may not know how your prayers are going to get answered but ALL you know is that the answer is on the way. Don't lose hope. Hold on! You are closer to your victory than you know. Our time is not God's time, but He's always right on time. Remember you have to help pray for one another. Pray and believe help stand in the gap for our brothers and sisters. God is working on your behalf and he is good all the time.

Be blessed.

Just a quick thought for today...

- -

Are you willing?

Lord I pray that you find me faithful and trustworthy. You have set me apart from this world that I may be your vessel and I pray that as I show your love, your fruit will spring forth as living water. For you have called us, equipped us and taught us about your loving kindness.

How do you want the Lord to find you? Are you willing to be a vessel used by Him? You have to be willing to allow God to use you to reach a lost and dying world. You have to sometimes get out of your comfort zone and go into the battlefield for Jesus. There are so many people around you who are hurting and lost. Ask God today to use you. Once you are a willing vessel, He can you use you in many ways. Romans 8:30 (GNT), "And so those whom God set apart, he called; and those he called, he put right with himself, and he shared his glory with them."

Be blessed.

Just a quick thought for today...

- -

Little moments

Lord, please remind me to enjoy every moment of every day. Your word states that I am not promised tomorrow, so I have to be ready today. James 4:14 (NASB), "Yet you do not know what your life will be like tomorrow. You are just a vapor that appears for a little while and then vanishes away."

Lord, I have made it my mission to give You my all and all,100 percent of me. You are my rock and my fortress and I will seek after You. Help me to keep my eyes on You looking straight ahead not straying to the right or left. It's so easy to look at my situation and get discouraged, but help me to have a smile on my face and joy in my heart at all times for this is the day that the Lord has made.

Be blessed.

- -

Who are you?

Would you describe yourself as an encourager or a faultfinder?

An encourager is a person who motivates and pushes and never points out the flaws or weaknesses in another person. Try to be an encourager, and speak to people as if they have already reached the level that you've set for them. A kind word goes a long way (I Thessalonians 5:11 NIV).

Five Qualities of a Great Encourager

Everyone can be a great encourager by developing
and nurturing five qualities.

1. A Genuine Heart for People. Encouragers demonstrate a real and loving concern for people.
2. An Empathetic Ear.
3. An Eye for Potential.
4. A Consistent Source of Hope.
5. Setting a Positive and Inspiring Example.

So, encourage someone today, be their biggest cheerleader by nurturing their potential.

Be blessed.

Just a quick thought for today...

- -

Take inventory

Do the people you hang around make a deposit or withdrawal in your love bank? Do you love to see them or do you try and hide from them? Maybe it's time to take inventory of those you hang around and start making changes. Make sure the ones you call "friends" uplift you and not drag you down. Those who we are closest to, should inspire us to be the best we can be.

Proverbs 13:20 (NLT) states, "Walk with the wise and become wise; associate with fools and get in trouble."

Be blessed.

Pity Party

If you are all completely honest, there has been a time or two where you have had a self -pity party. But it's time that you as believer rise up and shake off that 'woe is me' attitude and know where your self- worth comes from.

Look, I get it, —life is hard, and there are times when you would love to lay down and cry and just let the world pass you by while you're attending your little pity party. But that is not what God has intended for you.

Psalms 121:1-8 (KJV) reminds you where your help comes from:

"I will lift up mine eyes unto the hills, from whence cometh my help. My help cometh from the Lord, which made heaven and earth. He will not suffer thy foot to be moved: he that keepeth thee will not slumber. Behold, he that keepeth Israel shall neither slumber nor sleep. The Lord is thy keeper: the Lord is thy shade upon thy right hand. The sun shall not smite thee by day, nor the moon by night. The Lord shall preserve thee from all evil: he shall preserve thy soul. The Lord shall preserve thy going out and thy coming in from this time forth, and even for evermore."

When you get up this morning, dry your tears, wash your face and praise Jesus for the victory. God has a miracle with your name written all over it. You just have to believe and have faith.

Be blessed.

Just a quick thought for today...

- -

People pleasers

Do you try to please people? You bend over backwards to make sure you do the right things, say the right things, act the right way, all to get the approval of people. Why? People pleasing imprisons your heart and keeps you bound. Trying to please people is hard. They make you feel like you're never good enough or don't meet their standards and that leaves you feeling defeated.

You need to learn to be God pleaser instead of people pleaser. Chase after His heart, His ways and His approval; after all He is what matters. Learning to fear God over people frees you and you start believing that you are good enough and worthy of love. Life is too short to always be chasing the wrong people trying to make them like you. It's time to grow up, be the man or woman God has called you to be and start chasing after God's approval. Stop being a follower and learn to be a leader.

Galatians 1:10 (NIV) states, "Am I now trying to win the approval of human beings, or of God? Or am I trying to please people? If I were still trying to please people, I would not be a servant of Christ."

Who is more important people or Christ? I would rather have God's approval in my life and know that He is pleased with how I conduct myself rather than having man's approval. Don't get me wrong, I'm not saying we shouldn't care about what others think, I'm saying it's more important to care about what God thinks.

Be blessed.

- - - - - - - - - - - - - - - - - - - -

It ain't over

'It ain't over yet' (this song popped up in my memories).

No matter what your family or friends have said about your situation. No matter what the doctors have said about the test results. No matter what the bank has said about your finances, IT AIN'T OVER YET UNTIL GOD SAYS IT'S OVER. He has the final say in all things. Remember, God likes to work when your back is against the wall and the only way out is trusting in him.

Your life is in His hands and He will fulfill every promise He has made to you. It may not be in your timing or the way you want it, but God is faithful. You have to keep praying, believing and expecting. When it is supposed to be, it will happen. We serve on on-time God, he is never early or late but always on-time.

Be blessed.

Just a quick thought for today...

- -

Managing our emotions

You need to learn how to manage your emotions rather than letting your emotions managing you. Don't live your life by doing
what feels right, but make wise decisions. Your emotions can
be positive or negative and affects everyone around you. God
doesn't want anyone to be a slave to their feelings. There may be
times where you allow your feelings to take over. that's when you
need to take a step back from the situation, take a deep breath
and remember you ARE NOT defined by your current situation.
Life is like a roller coaster- you maybe up one minute and down
the next, but it's how you handle life's ups and down that others
can see God at work in your lives. In order to manage your emotions and your life, you need to ask God for His wisdom instead
of trusting your feelings. One of my favorite quotes by Frank
Outlaw expresses this principle well:

Watch your thoughts, they become words.
Watch your words, they become actions.
Watch your actions, they become habits.
Watch your habits, they become character.
Watch your character, it becomes your destiny.

Be blessed!!

Standing firm

People may think I'm crazy for trusting God for our house, but I have faith in knowing what He showed Reggie (my husband). I may not know when or how, but I believe it's coming. I thank you Lord for the faith to believe and trust in Your word.

God's word never returns void and His promises are yes and amen.

II Corinthians 1:20 (NKJV) reads "For all the promises of God in Him are Yes, and in Him Amen, to the glory of God through us."

No matter what you are trusting God for, stand on faith and believe that He will answer your prayers. This world needs to see and hear you, a Christian, praying in faith. You have sat back to long allowing Satan to stand in your way. So today, declare that you are taking back all of the promises that God has for you and your family that Satan has stolen or tried to block in Jesus' name! This is your year of jubilee!

Be blessed.

Just a quick thought for today...

Seasons

Lord help me to remember that You always take me through a time of preparation before my promotion and teach me to learn to be content in the season I am in. In this life, I may face difficult times, but You are there with me, taking each step with me, bearing my burdens. I need to remember it's always darkest just before dawn and my joy comes in the morning as long as I trust and believe in You.

"For his anger lasts only a moment, but his favor lasts a lifetime! Weeping may last through the night, but joy comes with the morning" (Psalms 30:5 NIV).

In due season our time will come, but for now, we will have to be content and not jealous of what others around have.

Be blessed.

Just a quick thought for today...

- -

Prayer

All are in need of prayer and sometimes you need others to stand in the gap for you when you don't know what or how to pray. So today I'm asking for anyone who reads this and if there is a prayer request, type it in the comment box and let's start a Facebook prayer line. I believe God can answer prayer no matter how big or small the request.

In Matthew 18:19-20 (ESV) it reads "Again I say to you, that if two of you agree on earth about anything that they may ask, it shall be done for them by My Father who is in heaven. For where two or three have gathered together in My name, I am there in their midst."

I know firsthand prayer works. I've seen it work within our family. When my daughter Hannah was five, she developed bruises all over body out of the blue. On Saturday, we had been on a trip with our church and she was not herself. She was tired, bruised and weak. On Sunday morning, when she woke up, I noticed there were additional bruising and my gut told me there was something terribly wrong. I took her took her to school on Monday and spoke with her teacher who urged me to call the doctor immediately. When the doctor's office opened, I called and took Hannah to see her pediatrician. His face went pale with one look at her and he ordered labs to be done urgently. Waiting was so hard. I called his office and when they answered their words cut me to my very core "I'm sorry Mrs. Widener but the doctor is going to have to give you these results." After what seems like forever, he called and his words were "where is

Hannah? You need to bring her to the children's hospital where a team of doctors are waiting for you." My heart sank and I knew it was bad. I immediately left work and on my drive home I begin to yell and scream at God telling him he could not have my baby girl but just as quickly as I was screaming, I begin to pray and we started a prayer chain with family and friends far and near. After arriving at the hospital, we were admitted to the children's oncology ward where we were told Hannah had leukemia, an enlarged spleen and a form of hepatitis and we could be there for 6 days to 6 weeks. The team of doctors immediately wanted to start treatment and I said no, we wanted to see what her labs said. All I can say is God is good. We were there exactly 24 hours and what had started out as leukemia God had changed to ITP (idiopathic thrombocytopenic purpura). A blood disorder that she out grew.

God had heard our cries, prayers and all the prayers of those surrounding us and he healed our baby girl. We had to watch her for five years, had labs drawn each year to make sure her platelet count was good, and to this day she is a healthy, happy young lady with no signs of ITP.

Be blessed

Just a quick thought for today...

- -

Be on guard

"The thief comes only to steal and kill and destroy. I came that they may have life and have it abundantly" (John 10:10 ESV).

Satan wants nothing more than to steal, kill and destroy. If you open up the door an inch he slips in and begins to tear down from the inside out. Guard your heart, mind, family and friend. Don't let Satan tear down what God has built up. Also, remember every action has a reaction, don't let others provoke you during conversations. Always be mindful of what you say because once the words have left your mouth, you can't take them back. Words hurt and when spoken out of hurt and anger does no one any good.

Be blessed.

Just a quick thought for today...

- -

Friends

As humans, there is a desire for friendship; -someone to hang out with, go out to eat, shopping, go to the beach or just to talk. You desire that one-on-one companionship. That one person who knows all about you, but is sworn to secrecy. Someone that will laugh or cry with you.

But what happens when your circle of friends gets bigger and they have other friends that they start to hang out with too in addition to spending time with you? Do we get mad and upset or are you happy because they've made new friends and because they are happy you should be too. Do you have room for others in your friendship circle? Christ desires to be your friend and He's a friend that will stick closer than a brother or sister. He will have your back when you feel the world is against you. He's the ONLY person you can talk to that will not slip up and tell someone else what's going on with you. He never judges you because His love is unconditional. Remember when you have friends you have a gift. The Bible tells us in Proverbs 17:17 (NLT), "A friend is always loyal, and a brother is born to help in time of need." Take a moment today and think about your friends, are you being the best friend you can?

Be blessed.

Just a quick thought for today...

- -

God's promises

How many times have you seen a beautiful rainbow in the sky and you immediately say thank you Lord? Every time I see a rainbow, I immediately think about God's promise to us and thank Him for His promises. God puts rainbows in the sky to show us a couple of things:

1. He is still in control
2. He will always make a way
3. His promises are still yes and amen

"I have placed my rainbow in the clouds. It is the sign of my covenant with you and with all the earth" (Genesis 9:13 NLT).

When God put the rainbow in the sky for Noah, He promised him He would never destroy the earth again by a flood. When things start to go crazy and you don't know how you are going to make it, ask God to show you a rainbow to let you know that everything is going to be okay.

Be blessed.

Just a quick thought for today...

- - - - - - - - - - - - - - - - - - - -

Work ethic

What is your work ethic like? Do you make sure you do your best even when no one is around or do you put on a show when people are watching?

The Bible tells us in Colossians 3:23 (NASB), "Whatever you do, do your work heartily, as doing it for the Lord and not for people."

God sees how you are and He knows if you put in 100% or if you put in just enough to get by. Our work ethic pertains to both the physical and spiritual side of life. Are you doing all you can for the kingdom of God or has He called you to do more and you are doing just enough to say I did what was asked of me? Let's face it, life is hard and we are faced with some hard choices but doing our best should never be one of them. Others depend on you to do your best and you should never give them less than what you would expect from someone else. So today I challenge you, whether you work outside of the home, work from home, stay at home with the children or go to school, give all you can. Go above your "normal" and let others know that you do care about the job you do. Your work ethic shows you truly care about the job you do and you take pride in it.

Be blessed.

Just a quick thought for today...

- -

I am not alone

Lord help me to remember that whatever I face today I do not face it alone. For You are with me at all times, through the good, bad, happy or sad times. Your word tells me in Isaiah 43:2, "When thou pass through the waters, I will be with you; and through the rivers, they shall not overflow you. When you walk through the fire, you shall not be burned, Nor shall the flame scorch you. *NKJV)"

I am so thankful that when faced with difficult times You have my back and I can call out Your name Lord. For You are my hiding place and You keep me safe.

Be confident today in knowing the God you serve is a mighty God and He will keep you safe from the storms and He will guide and direct you through this life.

Be blessed.

- -

God's got this

Never forget that God has your back. Just because man said it's impossible God tells you in His word in Matthew 19:26 (NIV), "With man this is impossible, but with God all things are possible."

What you're praying for may look like it's out of your reach but just remember God has the final say. It may not happen today, tomorrow, next week or even next month, but it will come to pass if you trust and believe that God has your best interest at heart. Everything happens in HIS timing not ours. Don't get discouraged or be disappointed in the "No" from man. God has a way of making that "no" from man turn into a yes. Just have faith, trust and believe. Gods got this!

Be blessed.

Just a quick thought for today...

- - - - - - - - - - - - - - - - - - - -

Be different

Our mission in this world is to show kindness to others around us. There is so much hate and negativity going on in this world right now. Go out of your way to show the love and kindness that you have been showed by Jesus. Let His light shine-forth from you today to everyone around you that you may be set apart from this world!! Jesus tells us in Romans 12:2 (NLT) "Don't copy the behavior and customs of this world, but let God transform you into a new person by changing the way you think. Then you will learn to know God's will for you, which is good and pleasing and perfect."

God wants us to take on His characteristics so others may see a difference in us apart from this world.

Be blessed

Praise through the trials

Don't ever get so wrapped up in your situation, whether good or bad, that you forget to praise God. In Job 2:9-10, Job was being tested and his health was not the best. His wife tells him to curse God and die, but Job looks at her and tells her that she was speaking like a foolish woman and asked did she forget that you can't have the blessings of God without going through trials.

Even in the midst of Jobs darkest hour, he remained steadfast and faithful to God, even with his speech. I'm sure when Jobs' wife said those words, she said them from the deepest despair and hurt, for she too had just lost her kids and everything they had worked so hard for. But I'm reminded of the song, "I'll praise you in this storm," that no matter what trials, tribulations or triumphs you face in this life, you need to praise God through every aspect of your life. Through it all, you can still hear that still small voice that can calms your storm just by speaking peace be still. Don't get so lost in the situation you're in that you forget to start praising your way to victory. Start doing your victory march and let the devil know he has no power and that you're going to praise God in the good times as well as the bad times. You are more than a conqueror through the blood of Jesus Christ. Romans 8:37 (NIV) "No, in all things we are more than conquerors through him who loved us."

Be blessed.

- -

Spend time with God

Do you ever look back at how far you've come and just say wow, that was nothing but God? If so, do you take the time to thank him?" He has your back and pushes you further than you ever thought you could go and way beyond your possibilities. God deserves your undivided attention at some point in your day. He's not asking that you spend ALL DAY with Him, but you should want to spend more quality time with Him than anyone else. Start getting up a little earlier to read His word, pray and seek Him or end your day with Him, but find a way to give God His time. He is the reason you are where you are today and He loves you more than anything, even enough to allow His only son to die on the cross for you. Today is a new page in your story of life, make God a priority and see how different things are. I'm not saying life will be a bed of roses with no trials, tribulations or problems, but with Him those things are easier to face. Take time today to reflect on how far He's brought you and remember to give God all the glory because without Him where you be today?

"With all my heart I will praise you, O Lord my God.
I will give glory to your name forever"
(Psalms 86:12 NLV).

Be blessed.

Just a quick thought for today...

- -

W.O.W

Make today W.O.W day:

W—walk in faith knowing
O—our life has a meaning in this
W—wonderful world

Get up and get moving for Christ. Let the world around you know that you're not ashamed of the gospel of Jesus Christ and you're going to proclaim it until you draw your final breath. Make life happen. Don't sit idle and watch life pass you by. You have meaning and a purpose and you were created for greatness!!

Be blessed

Just a quick thought for today...

- -

Control

Your mindset plays a major role in how your day goes. A negative mindset will always bring about chaos and hardships, but a positive mindset will bring clarity and victory. Only you can control your way of thinking.

I've always been taught that every action has a reaction. You can control how you allow this world and your surroundings to impact you, negative or positive. Life happens and going around looking down and defeated, will only ever leave you defeated. Allow yourself to see that God allows it to rain on the just and the unjust (Matthew 5:45) and understand that your current situation *DOES NOT DEFINE YOU OR YOUR FUTURE*, and allow yourself to start seeing and thinking positively. Everyone in this world faces trials and tribulations, but it's how you react to them that speaks volumes to those around us. An attitude of gloom, doom and agony is not a pretty picture.

Start everyday out by praying and asking God to help you see something good in every situation you face and learn that you're not alone and you're going to make it. Start speaking positively, place positive sayings around your home, car or office and learn to face life head on with a new attitude. Put a smile on your face because you are somebody special and you are loved. Stop believing the lies of the devil, he wants you to continue to be surrounded by negativity, but put him in his place which is under your feet. You are a warrior not a victim!

Be blessed.

Just a quick thought for today...

- -

Finding Favor

The praise team have been practicing a song called,
"For Your Glory" by Tasha Cobbs

The first verse says:

"Lord if I Find favor in Your sight
Lord, please Hear my hearts cry
I'm desperately waiting
To be where You are
I'll cross the hottest desert
I'll travel near or far"

This verse sits in my spirit daily. Are you truly desperate to be where Jesus is? Is He priority in your life? My desire is to find favor in His sight and earnestly seek Him every day.

I'm most thankful that I serve a living Savior who sees and loves me just the way I am and when I call out to Him, He hears my hearts cry. He has given me family and friends whom I love and I thank Him for daily. I challenge you today to make God your first priority in your life and watch the amazing things that start happening.

"With all my heart I want your blessings. Be merciful as you promised" (Psalms 119:58 NLT)

Be blessed.

- -

Gifts

I'm reminded of one of my pastor's sermons, he made a point that everything we have is a gift from God and we have to understand that we do not have the ability to do anything, it's only through Jesus that we are able to move, breath and operate.

Matthew 10:8 (KJV) states "...freely ye have received, freely give."

Today we need to give ALL we have to Christ and He will guide and direct us. "Trust in the Lord with all your heart and lean not on your own understanding; in all your ways submit to him, and he will make your paths straight" (Proverbs 3:5-6 NIV).

In the movie, *Facing the Giants*, the coach resolved that without God, his life, his coaching ability and team could not do anything. When he finally gave *everything,* every part of his life over to God it all turned around.

We have to trust that God is going to help us through every aspect of our life. I challenge you as well as myself, to give God everything and leave the results up to Him.

Be blessed.

- -

Laughter

At one point or another, you have lost your laughter. You get so wrapped up in what's going on around you that you forget to laugh. When's the last time you really laughed, and no I don't mean a little chuckle here or there, I mean a laugh that was contagious and afterwards your whole demeanor changed?

God created you to laugh and enjoy life. If you walk around with a frown on your face or a woe is me attitude, others may tend to stay away from you and avoid you at all cost. When you learn life is not always about you and your issues and you learn that it's okay to laugh and have fun that's when you allow the heart and emotions to heal. Find something about today that makes you smile or laugh. Even in the worst situations or the hardest of times, a memory can brighten up the moment and bring joy to your heart, even if it's for a just a minute. Learn to enjoy life and remember laughter is truly medicine for the soul.

"A happy heart is good medicine and a joyful mind causes healing, But, a broken spirit dries up the bones" (Proverbs 17:22 AMP)

Be blessed.

Just a quick thought for today...

- -

Rise Up

It's time that you as a believer rise up and shake off that woe is me attitude and know where our self-worth comes from. WE ARE GOD'S CHILDREN and there is nothing more precious than a child.

I get it, I really do, life is hard, I know this first hand and you would love to lay down and cry and just let the world pass you by as you attend and participate in your little pity party dance. But that is not what God has intended for you.

He has told you in His in Psalms 121:1-8 (ASV),

"I will lift up mine eyes unto the hills, from whence cometh my help. My help cometh from the Lord, which made heaven and earth. He will not suffer thy foot to be moved: he that keepeth thee will not slumber. Behold, he that keepeth Israel shall neither slumber nor sleep. The Lord is thy keeper: the Lord is thy shade upon thy right hand. The sun shall not smite thee by day, nor the moon by night. The Lord shall preserve thee from all evil: he shall preserve thy soul. The Lord shall preserve thy going out and thy coming in from this time forth, and even for evermore."

Get up this morning dry your tears, wash your face and praise Jesus for the victory!!! There is a miracle with your name written all over it, we just have to believe and have faith! I'm reminded of that song by Lauren Daigle, "I Will Trust You" when she says things may not always happen when I want them to, but I will still trust in you Lord,

Be blessed.

Just a quick thought for today...

- -

You will make it

Make the most of everyday. Take time to enjoy life. Learn to
laugh and smile!

There may be times when you allow situations or circumstances
around you dictate your way or your mood. You have to learn
that through each trial God is using it to teach life lessons.
Remember it won't rain always, the sun will shine again and you
will be stronger because of your trial. Begin each day with prayer
and ask God what does He have for you to learn today? When
you face each day with God, He has a way of making things
seem brighter no matter what you are facing.

So, when life gets tough, the tough keeps going. You WILL make
it through this, just keep your head lifted, a smile on your face, a
song in your heart and Jesus by your side.

"Be careful for nothing; but in everything by prayer and supplication with thanksgiving let your requests be made known
unto God. And the peace of God, which passeth all understanding, shall keep your hearts and minds through Christ Jesus"
(Philippians 4: 6-7 KJV).

Be blessed.

Your plans

What are your plans? How will your days go? Will you start each day out by dreading going to work or school? Or do you see this day as a fresh adventure? A new start to realize that God has woke you up and given you a brand-new opportunity to fulfill your dreams, the opportunity to become a better you, the opportunity to share His word with those around you. Or do you see this day as just another boring day filled with the same ole same ole?

Start today out by thanking God for waking you up (because some won't), for giving you purpose (because some have lost theirs), opening doors (some have closed), and allowing you the chance to make something new of yourself.

In Jeremiah 29:11(NIV) the Bible tells us "For I know the plans I have for you," declares the Lord, "plans to prosper you and not to harm you, plans to give you hope and a future.

He knows all about you and only wants the best for you.

Be blessed.

Just a quick thought for today...

- -

Something different

Let's try something a little different today. Let's try praying for one another instead of degrading or belittling each other or grumbling about one another.

In James 5:16 (NIV), "Therefore confess your sins to each other and pray for each other so that you may be healed. The prayer of a righteous person is powerful and effective."

Our words speak life or death and in the heat of the moment, what comes out of our mouths is truly what is in our hearts. What's in your heart today? Your words will match your actions and your actions will match what's in your heart. Be mindful and say a prayer for those around you today. You never know what they faced this morning before you saw them. Sometimes a simple smile or a sweet gesture will brighten even the darkest of moments. I pray you have a joyful day, filled with lots of great memories. It's time you make each moment count because you aren't promised the next one.

Love you.

Be blessed.

Thoughts?

Where do you allow your thoughts to come from? Is it from a positive or negative source? Your thoughts are what carries you through the day. Your thoughts are what keeps you happy, sad, mad or angry. Hebrews 4:12 (ESV) says,

"For the word of God is living and active, sharper than any two-edged sword, piercing to the division of soul and of spirit, of joints and of marrow, and discerning the thoughts and intentions of the heart".

Have you ever had a thought about something that truly made you happy? If so, it probably put a smile on your face and you were in a good mood. Or have you had a thought of something that angered you? If so, is probably put a frown on your face and your whole attitude changed to a hateful and mean mood. Maybe you've never given a thought about your thoughts, but they control your attitudes, your actions, your words, and your feelings. Why do you think Satan tries so hard to control your thought pattern? If he can control your thoughts then he can manipulate you. If a person has anger or suicidal thoughts, who do you think plants them there and continues to whisper in their ear until they can't hear anything else?

Your mind is where every thought pattern generates from and you have got to ask God to cover and protect your minds and your thoughts. Pray today for God to cover your mind and to give you good and happy thoughts. Let His love and joy control your emotions and let His light shine though you today.

Be blessed.

Just a quick thought for today...

- -

Examples

The Bible tells you to be like Joshua and make a bold stand for Jesus. In Joshua 24:15 (KJV), Joshua proclaims a bold statement when he says

"As for me and my house we will serve the Lord."

So thankful for my parents who took that stand and raised my brother and myself in church. Now, as adults having our own families, we have made that same decision. We have been blessed to have such an awesome Godly heritage that has been passed down for generations. And I pray that as our own children grow-up they will raise their families in church and make a difference for Christ. Our kids learn by our behavior. What example are you being for your family?

Be blessed.

- - - - - - - - - - - - - - - - - - -

God's love

If you could ever really capture how much God loves you, you would be overwhelmed. His love for you is unconditional, unending, everlasting, the rawest form of love! He sees you at the lowest and highest points of your life and yet He still loves you.

"Because of the Lord's great love, we are not consumed,
for his compassions never fail.
They are new every morning;
great is your faithfulness
(Lamentations 3: 22-23 NIV).

It is only because of the love of God that you are able to make it from day to day. God only wants the best for His children and you should not settle for anything less. Take a moment today to just thank God for His love and provisions, after all He woke you up again this morning and gave you a new day to begin living a life filled with joy, happiness, peace and a love that overflows on to others. It's so much harder to try to live with hate, anger, bitterness and an unforgiving attitude!!

Be blessed.

Just a quick thought for today...

- -

True Warrior

As I look at all the pictures of parents taking their kids back to school and getting them settled in, I remembered the last time we took a trip to Clemson with Hannah. She accomplished so much during her time at Clemson (she was a true warrior). It was not an easy road for her. Most people can look back and say that their college experience was the best time of their lives, but what I can say about Hannah's experience is I'm thankful that God kept His hand of protection around her. She is truly a survivor. I spent many nights praying and calling her name out before the throne of Jesus and asking him to wrap His arms around Hannah. I would listen to her beg to transfer back to USCA and I'd have to tell her not to let others actions destroy her dream. Her college life was not easy socially, but academi-cally she excelled. Listen, my baby girl was on the Dean's list and the President's list each semester! I can say that through all of the trials and tribulations she faced she stayed rooted and grounded in Christ even when she felt like she couldn't make it another step. She pressed in and continued her journey, but here we are, reaping the reward of her hard work. She is a graduate of Clemson University and a second-year teacher at Millbrook Elementary.

I said all of that to say this, as I sit here, I can't help but wonder how many of you are striving toward your Christian goals.? Your goal is making heaven your home. You may face trials and tribulations along your way but if you are steadfast and keep your eyes on Jesus, you too will reach your goal. Even though you may face obstacles along your way, never let those obstacles keep you down; get up, shake it off and move forward with Christ. Always remember that even in great trials, God is faithful and He is the one person you can completely trust to have your back at all times.

"These things I have spoken to you, that in me you might have peace. In the world you shall have tribulation: but be of good cheer; I have overcome the world" (John 16:33 NKJV).

Be blessed.

Just a quick thought for today...

- -

What's your view

As I was listening to Priscilla McGruder sing, "Heavens Point of View," I started to think about how many times we are faced with what looks like a mountain to us, but to God it's just a hill. You may get so wrapped up in your situation that you forget that the God you serve can move mountains. He can turn any situation around at any time. There may be times you allow that mountain to defeat you when you should have been on your knees praying, trusting, and believing that God would take care of it. When He doesn't move in your time or on your terms, don't think He's not listening because you serve a God that hears your cries 24/7, 365 days a year. He never sleeps, he never slumbers, His line is not disconnected, he doesn't' go on vacation, He's always there looking down from Heaven's point of view. He sees you when you have tears streaming down your cheeks, He hears you crying in the dark, He feels every emotion you feel and He's fighting your battles when you are tired. The Bible tells says in Isaiah 40:31 (NLT), "But those who trust in the LORD will find new strength. They will soar high on wings like eagles. They will run and not grow weary. They will walk and not faint."

So, the next time you're faced with a situation that you don't know how to handle or fix, remember that from Heaven's point of view it's not an impossible mountain, but a hill that you can climb as long as you put your trust in God, for He will see you through.

Be blessed.

Just a quick thought for today...

- -

Struggles

Do you struggle with insecurities?
I am willing to be honest, and say yes I do.

I know that within my own self I am nothing, but through Christ I can do mighty things. I can be bold, fearless and believe God for big things when my confidence is solely in Him.

Ephesians 3:20 says that God is able to "do superabundantly, far over and above all that we [dare] ask or think [infinitely beyond our highest prayers, desires, thoughts, hopes, or dreams]" (AMP).

He's waiting on you to take your eyes off of your circumstances and put them on Him, trusting that He will do great things. Don't let your insecurities keep you from doing great things through Christ.

"I can do all things through Christ who strengthens me" (Philippians 4:13 ESV).

Without Him you are nothing but with Him you are a mighty-warrior. Trust Him today and see what he can do.

Be blessed.

- -

Pressing on

How often, when you are going through a battle or a storm in your life, do you forget your praise? Every morning I wake to a song, one in particular, "I Raise a Hallelujah" on my mind and in my spirit. The lyrics to this song stir my spirit and make me feel ashamed.

How often do you forget that your God is bigger than anything you face? When you truly have the faith and belief that He can *DO ANYTHING*, even the IMPOSSIBLE, that is when you draw closer to Him.

In Matthew 19:26 (NIV) Jesus was speaking to a crowd and looked at them and said, "With man this is impossible, but with God all things are possible."

Today if you are faced with what seems to be the impossible start praising your way to victory and know that God's fighting for you. Start praising and singing the way Paul and Silas did when they were in prison. They were bound by chains but when they begin to praise the chains fell away and they were set free.

Be blessed.

Living in the past

Are you living in the past? Is it that you are afraid to let go of what was and embrace the now? Sometimes you miss out on the great things that are happening around you because you are too wrapped up in your old memories to allow yourselves to make new memories. Don't get me wrong, I hold on dearly to some of my past memories and I will treasure them forever but I've learned in order to move forward with my life, I have to be willing to allow myself to make room for new memories and learn that time waits for no one and God has granted me and you the opportunities to adapt to the world around us, not to be conformed to this world but to be set apart from it. Even though this world is rapidly changing, you have to be willing to change with it. For example, growing up all I listened to was southern gospel. I did not care for contemporary music, but even though we were raised in the same house, Jody (my brother) preferred contemporary Christian, over southern gospel. As I grew older and we (Reggie and myself) became youth leaders in the teenage class, I found myself learning to be open to their music and I saw how what I thought was horrible music was actually great music and I now love them both. I've watched my own kids as they listen to their style of music (contemporary Christian) with their hands raised worshipping Jesus. For that reason, I am blessed that Jesus accepts our worship no matter what music we are listening to at the time as long as our worship is done with a sincere heart.

So today hold on to your precious memories of childhood, but be willing to make new ones. Don't be left looking at old pictures wondering what if. Get out and embrace the now and learn to enjoy what God has done and is doing amongst His people. You might find yourself letting go and learning to enjoy life again. The Bible tells says in Philippians 3:13-14 (AMP),

"Brothers and sisters, I do not consider that I have made it my own yet; but one thing I do: forgetting what lies behind and reaching forward to what lies ahead, I press on toward the goal to win the [heavenly] prize of the upward call of God in Christ Jesus."

In these last days God is stirring His people, getting ready to rapture them out of this vile and wicked world. Don't miss what God is doing now because you're stuck in the past saying "we've always done it this way." The one thing you can be assured of is God's words was, is and always will be the same, not one jot or tittle will pass until it has all been fulfilled. Our methods may be a little different, but our goals are the same and this one thing remains the constant, Jesus Christ was born, crucified and rose again to save you from a devil's hell so that you may be saved from your sins and live with Him forever.

Be blessed.

- -

What is your character

You cannot control the words or actions of others, but you can control your responses. There will always be someone who will lie to you, say horrible things about you, or betray you, but it's how you handle the situation that speaks volumes about who you are, what your character is.

In I Samuel 17, is the story of how Goliath taunted King Saul and his army and every one of Saul's men were scared to face him. One little shepherd boy, who brought food and supplies for his brothers, heard the giant and was angered by Goliath's disrespect towards God so he volunteered to fight him. He took five smooth stones, a sling and his boldness from the Lord and killed the giant with one stone from his slingshot. He knew he had God on his side and he had nothing to fear.

With God fighting your battles, you have nothing and no one to fear. It does you no good to lose control over what someone says or does to and toward you. Your retaliation makes you stoop to their level and causes others to lose respect for you. Some battles are better fought on your knees in prayer and letting God do your fighting. He can protect your character better than you can. Learn to let go and let God take over the situation. You just need to thank Him for having your back.

Be blessed.

Just a quick thought for today...

- -

Ordinary or Extra?

How many times have you thought and maybe even prayed, I wish God would use me and show me what's my purpose in life. When you come to Christ, you have to come with a willing heart and be an open vessel. You have to pour all of yourself out in order for Him to fill you up with His spirit. When you give God your ordinary, He can turn it into something extraordinary. God can use anyone or anything. If He used a donkey in Numbers 22:28 to speak to Balaam, He can surely use you

Will you give God your ordinary and allow Him to give you the something *extra*?

Be blessed.

New Creation

"Therefore, if any man be in Christ, he is a new creature: old things are passed away; behold, all things are become new" (II Corinthians 5:17 KJV).

Have you ever really stopped and thought about that verse?

You are made new every day. God is shaping you into what He wants you to be when you completely surrender your life and your ways to Him. He continues to add and take away, shape and mold us every day. If you are not growing, you are dead. A garden, for example, has to be watered and pruned in order to produce fruits and veggies and if it's not taken care of, it will wither and die. God has to continuously prune and feed you His word for you to produce good fruits. If you are never growing, you can become stagnant and you spew out toxins to those around you. Your daily prayer should be, Lord make me new today.

Be blessed.

Just a quick thought for today...

- -

Faithful

I don't know what you are praying for or what answers you need, but I know a God who is faithful and just. He hears your cries in the dark and wipes your tears as they fall. He's one that will stick closer than a brother and walk with you through the fire. He will never leave you or forsake you. He's an on-time God. He's never early or late and when you pray and His answer is no, it just means He has something better in store for you. So today don't give up, you may be on the brink of the answer you are looking for, on the verge of your miracle.

"Never stop praying" (I Thessalonians 5:17 NLT)

Be blessed.

Just a quick thought for today...

Where is your hope?

God's answers are always worth waiting on. What are you praying and hoping for? Don't give into doubt or fear. Keep praying and expecting your miracle to happen. Remember God is faithful to His promises and what He has said. He will be faithful and just.

I know that God has promised my family "our year of jubilee."

I may not see certain things with my physical eye, but I know God is working on my behalf. He is our anchor, our rock, our steadfast hope and He will not let us down.

Real hope is not a wishy-washy, vague, "let's just wait and see what happens" attitude; It's believing and trusting that what God promised, He will do.

So today don't give up, your miracle is on the way!!

"And so, Lord, where do I put my hope? My hope is in you."
(Psalms 39:7 NLT)

Your only hope is in Him.

Be blessed.

- -

Waiting on a breakthrough

I came across something I had posted from another Facebook page several years back, and as I started to read it again, it was as if I was revisiting a promise that was spoken over Reggie and myself many years ago. It's from the "Woman of God...I cover you," Facebook page:

"God says, 'you have been waiting for this breakthrough for years now. At times it seemed as though it was not going too happened. But I kept it alive when it seemed all but dead. You did not give up. You kept the faith. No one really knows how much you have gone through because of it. Now it is your due season. I AM about to send your breakthrough. Delayed, but not denied!"

And the last line of that says: "DELAYED, BUT NOT DENIED" let me say that again...

DELAYED, BUT NOT DENIED!

I don't know about you, but there have been so many times I have prayed and thought, today is the day I'm going to get my breakthrough and it passes by. Friend, I am here today to tell you don't give up. Just because your time has not come doesn't mean it's not. God's timing is not our timing and His ways are not our ways, but that delay may mean something better than what you are praying for is on the way. The Bible says in Ephesians 3:20 (ESV),

"Now to him who is able to do far more abundantly than all that we ask or think, according to the power at work within us."

You have to trust and believe that God is working on your behalf even though you can't see it or feel it. God always has your best interests at heart and you have to learn to let go and trust Him. He is not a God that can lie for if He said it, He will bring it to pass. Keep praying and believing. You've come too far to stop now. I'll pray for you and you pray for me that whatever God has for us, He will bring it to pass and those around us will know that it was God's handy work and not ours. Pray, ask and believe.

Be blessed.

Just a quick thought for today...

- -

He holds tomorrow

Do you ever just want to crawl back in bed and cover up your head? Nothing seems to be going your way from the time your feet hit the floor?

I've been there, but rise up, shake the devil off and let him know that today is the day that the Lord has made and you will rejoice and be glad no matter what you face (Psalms 118:24). His mercies are new and fresh this morning and no matter what happened yesterday, He's woke you up and is giving you another day to make things right. Don't let today pass you by without thanking Jesus for His love and forgiveness and don't let another day go by without mending broken relationships. You never know what tomorrow will hold.

Be blessed.

Just a quick thought for today...

- -

What's important?

Have you stopped to think about what is really going on around you? And what I mean is, have you thought about that this may be God's way of saying to you, 'I need to you to focus on what's important.'

We have seen more pastors doing live feeds on Facebook (which I think has been awesome). We need Gods word spread to everyone. Jobs are closing, schools are closed, restaurants are only open for takeout, movie theaters are closed and the public has been asked to stay home.

I understand that this coronavirus is horrible, but maybe instead of looking at this as a horrible time, start looking at it as time we've been given to spend true quality time seeking after God and more time to spent with our families. A lot of us, myself included, have made our jobs a high priority and that's okay when it's put into perspective. Yes, I know bills have to be paid, groceries purchased, all the basic necessities in order to live, but some people are working so much they miss out on what's truly important, family time.

I understand during this horrific situation of things shutting down money is going to be tight, but take the time to play games with your family, actually carry-on real conversations and listening intently to what is being said. Engage in family Bible studies, pray together as a family, draw strength from one another during this time, and ask your kids how this is affecting them. We will get through this hard time but it's going to take us looking to God for His protection.

"He that dwelleth in the in the secret place of the most-High, shall abide under the shadow of the Almighty. I will say of the Lord, He is my refuge and my fortress: my God; in him will I trust" (Psalm 91:1-2 KJV)

He is your refuge and He will keep and protect you as long as you dwell in Him.

Continue to pray for our leaders, as they make decision's they think are best for this country and pray for those on the front-line, the healthcare workers.

Be blessed.

Satan is a liar

Satan wants nothing more than to steal, kill and destroy.

The thief comes only to steal and kill and destroy. I came that they may have life and have it abundantly (John 10:10 ESV).

If we open up the door an inch, the devil slips in and begins to tear you down from the inside out. Guard your hearts, minds, families and friends. Don't let Satan tear down what God has built up. And remember every action has a reaction. Don't let others provoke you during conversations. Always be mindful of what you say because once the words have left your mouth you can't take them back. Words hurt and spoken out of hurt and anger does no one any good.

Be blessed.

Just a quick thought for today...

- -

Chosen People

No matter what season of life you are in right now, God's Grace will keep you. For every season has its own beauty and burden. As long as you keep your eyes on the creator, the sustainer, the way maker, the miracle worker, the promise keeper, your light in the darkness, you will make it through. The Bible tells says in Romans 8:28 ESV,

"And we know that for those who love God all things work together for good, for those who are called according to his purpose."

Always remember you are a child of the most-High King, a chosen people and He is working behind the scenes on your behalf. Even when you don't see or feel it, He's there.

Be blessed.

Just a quick thought for today...

Favor for my life

Lord, help me to remember that I serve the God of a break-through as described by David.

I believe that even now you are working on my behalf and my breakthrough is just around the next sunrise!!

Sometimes your life may seem dark, but you have to remember that joy comes in the morning

"For His anger *is but for* a moment, His favor *is for* life; Weeping may endure for a night, But joy *comes* in the morning" (Psalms 30:5 NKJV).

With that joy comes peace that is so sweet. Thank you, Lord for being my joy and peace.

Be blessed.

Just a quick thought for today...

True Blessings

When was the last time you stopped and just thanked God for His many blessings? I was listening to an old southern gospel song by Jeff and Sheri Easter, "Thank you Lord for Your Blessings on Me," and it got me to thinking; so many times, you are looking for the "next best thing" that you forget to be happy with what you have. You may not have the biggest or nicest house but we have a roof over your head, you may not be eating fancy gourmet meals, but you have food on your tables and while you may not be wearing the newest most popular clothes or shoes, you aren't walking around naked and barefoot.

So many times, you take what you have for granted that you get so wrapped up in your own wants you forget your blessings. There are those around you at work, school or church that are less fortunate than you are and would love to have what you have. They have no clue where they will sleep tonight or where their next meal is coming from or even if they will have a decent set of clothes to wear, but they are thankful for what little they do have.

Don't misunderstand me, having nice things is not wrong, we all desire them, but when your happiness comes from your possessions, then you are never truly happy. You never know the road others are having to travel or why things have happened to them but you need to remember it's only by the grace of God, you are not homeless and hungry.

The Bible tells says in Matthew 25:40 NKJV,

"And the King will answer and say to them, 'Assuredly, I say to you, inasmuch as you did it to one of the least of these My brethren, you did it to Me."

The next time you start feeling sorry for yourself because you don't have the latest and greatest, take a moment, and look around and see what you do have and tell the Lord thank you for the blessing you have given me. Lastly, when given the opportunity, help someone in need. You will never experience the joy of giving until you help those less fortunate. Life is not about serving ourselves but it's about serving others. When we, as a nation, learn to humble ourselves and put others first, then we will learn to live in unity.

Be blessed.

- -

At Jesus' feet

How many times do you find yourselves just wanting to be at the feet of Jesus, but the cares and burdens of this life seem to always get in the way?

There is a song that I sing with my choir and the second verse goes like this:

"It's hard to understand when life seems so unfair why I'm carrying this load that I'm not meant to bear but you said that in your word PEACE could be found if I could find the courage just to lay my burdens down." There are times when you get so wrapped up in everyday trials and tribulations that you forget to go to the master, your burden bearer and lay all of your troubles at His feet.

He tells us in Matthew 11:28 ESV,"Come to Me, all who are weary and heavy-laden, and I will give you rest."

Sometimes you have to take a few moments and just say: Father, I need you and your sweet peace to be with me today. I'm not sure how things will work out, but God I can't wait to see how YOU work it out. I come to you with all my burdens, heartaches, fears and troubles and I lay them at your feet because God there is no-place I would rather be than at your feet.

He hears His children when you cry out to Him and He comes running to your rescue every time. It may not be on your time but He's never early and He's never late. Remember this today—you are never alone, God is always with you, even in those times where you feel like He's millions of miles away. All you need to do is reach up and let the master take control and He will wrap His loving arms around you and give you such sweet peace.

Be blessed.

What's your choice?

In this day and time, we sometimes have a hard time being able to differentiate between Christians and non-believers. God has called us to be holy. Not to only look holy but He's called us to be faithful not just look faithful. As a Christian, you are to be different, your talk should be different, and your walk should be different. You can't walk hand in hand with the devil on Monday through Saturday and expect God to use you on Sunday. I'm not saying you are to act as if you are better than anyone because you are not. You are a sinner saved by grace and the world should be able to see that there is a difference. The Bible tells us Matthew 6:24 24 ESV,

"No one can serve two masters; for either he will hate the one and love the other, or he will be devoted to the one and despise the other. You cannot serve God and mammon [money, possessions, fame, status, or whatever is valued more than the Lord]."

God is calling you to make a choice. What's your choice? You are called to make a difference, not be part of the problem.

Be blessed.

Jesus in me

In this world I want others to be able to see Jesus in me more than anything. My desire is to be a light to others in this dark world and to lead others to Christ. Many times, you may find yourself putting other things before God that He gets lost in the shuffle of your life, placed on the back burner until a situation comes about and He's your last resort. You make excuses as to why God's not a priority in your life.

The Bible tells us in Matthew 6:33 NLT,

"Seek the Kingdom of God above all else, and live righteously, and he will give you everything you need."

I try to make sure that I start my day off by reading the Bible, doing my devotion and prayer. Does this happen every single morning? NO, but I can tell a difference when I don't do it I am human just like you, reading this and I too have days where "life happens" and things go awry and that's when I have to stop take a moment, slip away and pray.

No matter what the situation, I always try to let others see Jesus in me. I try my best to stay calm and not let this world get the best of me and yes that's hard especially in this day and age, where everyone feels "entitled or offended." In situations like that, this world is watching, waiting for you to slip up and be just like them, instead of being set apart from this world allowing others to see Jesus. When my time has passed, my hope is that I have lived a life pleasing to God and that others will say she

walked the walked and talked the talk and she lived her life pro-
claiming the gospel of Jesus Christ through the life she lived.
I hope my family and friends would be able to say, she was a
prayer warrior who loved the Lord more than anything else. We
only have the dash between the day we are born until the day
we die. What will that dash mean for you when it's your time?
What will others say about you? Take time today and ask Jesus
to let others see Him in you.

Be blessed.

Trusting God

In this world, there is a daily serving of headlines dishing out bad news, of seemingly unending turmoil that creates a constant unsettledness. It's easy to allow stress, fear and anxiety to overtake us. But the Bible says, you can be free from all that turmoil and live a peaceful life but you have to stay in His word, praying and seeking God. In Isaiah 26:3(ESV) says, "You will keep him in perfect peace, whose mind is stayed on You, because he trusts in You."

You have to trust that God has things under control even when you may not see it. His will and plan are perfect. You may have to walk through the fire, but He's with you and will not allow you to be burnt.

In Philippians 4:6-7 (NIV), He commands His children: "Do not be anxious about anything, but in every situation, by prayer and petition, with thanksgiving, present your requests to God. And the peace of God, which transcends all understanding, will guard your hearts and your minds in Christ Jesus".

So how do you deal with the everyday stress, fears and anxiety? You lay them at the feet of Jesus. He can handle more than you were created to handle and in laying them down, you are letting Him know that "I trust you through all of my problems and cares of this life and I know you are always with me."

So today, start trusting the One who created you and who is the only One that can give you perfect peace.

Be blessed.

Just a quick thought for today...

- -

Meditate on His word

There is a difference between reading God's word and meditating on God's word. When you meditate on His word, you think, and think seriously, about what they're reading. You're asking God to reveal Himself to you through what you read. The more you meditate on God's Word, the stronger you'll become and the more easily you'll win the victory.

Ask God today to fill your life with a hunger for more of Him and His word, so that in everything you may prosper. Don't just read God's word out of habit, read His word to draw closer to God. Start this week off right.

"My eyes are awake through the night watches, that I may meditate on Your word" (Psalms 119:148 NKJV).

Be Blessed.

Just a quick thought for today...

- -

Created in His image

The Bible says, you are made in the image of God. Are you being his reflection? Or do you need to make changes? How you handle yourself in situations allows the real you to be seen, whether positive or negative, you have the power to control who you are.

My prayer for myself is that I always show the love and spirit of Christ. I know that being the woman God intended me to be will cost me friendships and relationships, but in the end when I stand before God, I want to hear him say "Well done, good and faithful servant: thou hast been faithful over a few things, I will set thee over many things; enter thou into the joy of thy Lord (Matthew 25: 23 KJV).

Be blessed.

Just a quick thought for today...

- -

Free from Guilt

In one of my devotions, I was reading about how the fear and guilt of the past keep us from the ministry that God has for us to do today.

Like most of us, you have a past, some more painful and worse than others, but the Bible reminds you in Romans 3:23-24 (KJV), for all have sinned and come short of the glory but are made free through the blood of Jesus. You no longer have to allow Satan to throw your past in your face and when you dwell on the sins of your past, you are allowing Satan to win. He knows if he can keep your mind on your past then you can't focus on what God has for you now. Satan steals your joy, peace and tries to bring complete destruction to your life. God says in His word that He is a just God who forgives freely when you ask and loves you unconditionally and throws your sins, your past in the sea of forgetfulness as far as the east is from the west. So, the next time Satan tries to remind you of your past, you remind him of his future. According to the book of Revelations you win! So, I urged you today to start living in the forgiveness of God and leave the past in the past where it belongs.

Be blessed.

Just a quick thought for today...

- -

He has called you

If God has called you to do a job then He will equip you. You are
His handy work and He is always molding and shaping you in
His likeness. The Bible tells us in Philippians 1:6 (NLT), "And I
am certain that God, who began the good work within you, will
continue his work until it is finally finished on the day when
Christ Jesus returns."

He will never lead you to an unfamiliar place without making
provisions for you. When you step out on faith, you have to trust
that God has made a way, even when you don't understand
where He is leading you. You have to trust that his plan is better
than ours.

Be blessed.

- -

Are you sincere

Are you sincere when you say or do things for others? Does it come straight from the heart with no expectations for anything in return? Or do you do things expecting them to give or say something back?

If you do not have a sincere heart and you are only doing or saying things for show trying to win man's approval, then what good have you done? Are you really showing the love of Christ if you are expecting something in return? When you give out of the abundance of the heart then it's sincerely giving.

"At this present time your abundance being a supply for their need, so that their abundance also may become a supply for your need, that there may be equality" (II Corinthians 8:14 NASB 1995).

So today give that sweet compliment or buy someone something with no expectations of receiving anything in return. Be a cheerful giver!!

Be blessed.

Just a quick thought for today...

- -

By the grace of God

Are you dreading going to work today? That job that you don't want to go to is an answer to someone else's prayer who's unemployed. That house you hate is an answer to someone who's homeless. That beat up car you can't stand to drive is an answer to someone's prayer who has to walk everywhere. The next time you see someone who's down on their luck, remember it's only by the grace of God that you are not in the same position. Everyone who's unemployed, homeless, carless, is not a bad person. We are commanded in the Bible in Matthew 7:12 (NIV) "So in everything, do to others what you would have them do to you, for this sums up the Law and the Prophets."

When you learn to treat others with respect, no matter what their situation or status quo that is when you will learn, you are one bad situation away from being in their shoes. Always remember God created all humans equal and no matter what position you have in society, you are still on even ground when we kneel before the cross.

Be blessed.

- -

Your kids need you

Be there for your kids. As I see other kids playing in sports, I realize just how much I miss watching my son play football. He was an amazing defensive and offensive player and I loved cheering him on every Friday night. It didn't matter if we were playing at home or away, I was at every game and he never doubted that I wouldn't be in those stands.

In this world, if you do not show your kids you support them, this world will be there giving them the wrong support, so if your child participates in sports or if they are involved in any school/church extra- curricular activities, you need to be there cheering them on. When they look back on these memories the one-thing they should be able to say is that you were there every time and they knew they could count on you. You should be their biggest cheerleader!

"Children are a gift from the LORD; they are a reward from him "(Psalms 127:3 NLT).

Time is too precious and the one thing you can never get back. You can make more money, but we can't make extra hours, minutes or seconds in the day. Once this day has passed, you will never get it back. We only have our kids for a season, then their grown and living their own lives, don't let the world influence them.

Be blessed.

Just a quick thought for today...

- - - - - - - - - - - - - - - - - - - -

Marriage

When you enter into the holy communion of marriage, you leave your parents and become one with your spouse. I heard our pastor say in one of his sermons that there is no other relationship that the Bible tells us that we become one.

"AND THE TWO SHALL BECOME ONE FLESH; so they are no longer two, but one flesh" (Mark 10:8 ESV).

Your relationship with your spouse is the most important relationship you should have other than your relationship with Christ, He should always be first in your lives and then your spouse. The way you treat one another shows your kids what type of spouse they are looking for. If you are constantly degrading your spouse in front of your children, then they will grow up to believe it's okay to talk that way about their spouse.

Husbands you should be teaching your sons how to treat their future wife by loving their mother with all of your heart and treating her as your queen. When you do this, you are also showing your daughters how their future husband should treat them. Your kids are watching how you act, how you talk and what you do. Show them the proper way to live their lives with others and how they should treat others. After all they learn from your behavior.

The proper order for your lives should be Jesus first, your spouse second, our kids third and all others after that. Remember, Christ should be the center of every relationship and as long as He is, all other relationships will be on point.

Be blessed.

Just a quick thought for today...

- -

A big God

What a mighty big God you serve. When you feel like your prayers aren't being heard, be confident that the God you serve hears the simplest prayer and moves on His time. There is an old song that tells you "His eye is on the sparrow, and I know He watches over me."

Look at how small a sparrow. If God cares about what happens to the smallest bird, how much more does He care about you. He is a *BIG* God and He loves you so much and even though He doesn't always answer when you want Him to, He's listening. Sometimes when He's delaying His answers, it's because He has something far greater than you could ever imagine. Ephesians 3:20 (NKJV) says, "Now to Him who is able to do exceedingly abundantly above all that we ask or think, according to the power that works in us."

He's working on your behalf even when you can't see it or feel it. Trust that He is for us and not against us.

Be blessed.

- -

Family

What does your family mean to you? When you think of your family does your heart swell with love and pride or does your heart hurt with pain and disappointment?

Family doesn't always mean those who are blood kin or related to you. It can mean those friends who are closer than your flesh and blood. But whichever it is, always remember that family is family and no matter what, you love one another.

When you get together with family, do you have a great time filled with lots of love and hugs and sweet memories? Or do you leave feeling hurt and pain?

God can heal your heart so you can love your family even during the hard times. The Bible tells us in Proverbs 18:24 (CEV), "Some friends don't help, but a true friend is closer than your own family."

Always remember to love the family that God has given you because one day He's going to need them back.

Be blessed...

Just a quick thought for today...

- -

A New Thing.

God is doing a new thing in these last days, He is calling
out to His people to be set them apart from this world and
trust in Him.

In Isaiah 43:20 (AMP), God tells his people to "Listen carefully,
I am about to do a new thing, Now it will spring forth; Will you
not be aware of it? I will even put a road in the wilderness, Rivers
in the desert."

This world is getting ready to see the hand of God move in ways
they have never seen. Be ready for what God is doing, make sure
you keep your eyes open, your heart pure, and your life right in
the eyes of the Lord.

Be blessed.

Just a quick thought for today...

- -

Life is too short

Life is so short and we as a people are too busy complaining about what offends us. It's time for people to grow up and learn to love one another because in Heaven we're not going be separated by race, color, creed or denomination. God created us all whether you like it or not, He doesn't choose one over the other.

"Very truly I tell you, no servant is greater than his master, nor is a messenger greater than the one who sent him" (John 13:16 NIV).

We are all created in God's image and we were all created to worship Him and Him alone. Each of our lives have value and when we look at a person and decide they are less valuable because of the way they look, we are saying that what God created doesn't matter. Make today a new day and start looking at people through God's eyes and not through your own. You may be surprised to see what beauty He has truly created.

Be blessed

Brace yourself

I was listening to a pastor talk about dreams he had and how they were from the Lord and how God was telling him to "brace himself." As a Christian, you better be bracing yourself with the word of God and prayer. Things going around you today is Bible prophecy coming true. The Bible says in Matthew 24:7 ESV, "For nation will rise against nation, and kingdom against kingdom. And there will be famines, pestilences, and earthquakes in various places."

You've come too far to allow Satan to destroy you from the inside out. God is calling for an army to rise up and you are part of that army. Now is not the time to give up, but a time to stand firm and put on the whole armor of God.

"Put on the full armor of God, so that you can take your stand against the devil's schemes" (Ephesians 6:11 NIV).

Brothers and sister, you need to pray and seek God like never before. Don't allow the things of this world like hate, greed, animosity, division, wrath, vengeance or any other things to take you over and harden your heart. He gives you this commandment in John 15:12 (ESV) "This is my commandment, that you love one another, as I have loved you."

Be blessed.

- -

Overwhelmed

I don't know about you, but there are days where I feel like I am completely overwhelmed by all that going on around me and all the things I have to do. We live in an all-or-nothing society that says I need to look, act, think, and speak perfectly or just throw in the towel and stop trying altogether and that in itself can become so overwhelming.

Your life can become one big cycle of "routine" that you forget to actually live your life and you begin taking so much for granted that when something comes along it can throw you off course, and you don't know how to handle it. You need to learn to slow down and live the life that God has designed for you, enjoy each moment and cherish each little memory. It's okay not to be perfect, it's okay not to look your very best every day, it's okay to act a little crazy at times and it's okay to take time out for yourselves. The world will still go on if you learn to slow down and relax and enjoy life. You are important and you have to take care of you if you want to be here for everyone else. So, don't let the cares of this life get you so boggled that you forget what is important.

God gave you this life to live not to struggle. So, the next time you feel as if the weight of this world is overtaking you, step back and breath and remember *this too shall pass* and I can do all things through Christ who strengthens me (Philippians 4:13 NKJV).

Be blessed.

Just a quick thought for today...

- -

The word of God

Is the word of God rooted deep within your heart?

Do you know the scripture when others need you to help them?

You have to make sure that God's word is planted in the soil of your lives and that if and when the time comes that your Bible is taken from you, you know His word. The Bible is your life line, it's your manual for how you are supposed to live your lives. You have often heard it said that out of the heart the mouth speaks. So, whatever you have planted within your heart, it's going to come out. I urge you today to start reading and learning His word. Get it deep within your spirit and allow it to penetrate every part of your life. Let it become alive within you, that you want more and more of it. Let it become a habit you cannot do without.

Be blessed.

Just a quick thought for today...

- - - - - - - - - - - - - - - - - - - -

Who is God to you?

Who is God to you? In one of my devotions, the author brought out how throughout the Bible God had many names for different people but each describing the character of God. In the beginning, he was the creator of heaven and earth. To Moses, he was the I Am when he went to Pharaoh. To Abraham and Isaac, he was the ram in the bush. To the three Hebrew boys in the fiery furnace, he was the fourth man in the fire. To Daniel in the lions den, he was the one who shut the lions mouths. Throughout the Bible we read how God made himself known to many in different ways but the ultimate fulfillment of God's revelation can be found in the person of Jesus Christ who was Yeshua incarnate in the flesh. The beginning and the end, the Alpha and Omega, the first and the last. During your times of need who is God to you? Is he your everything or is he your go to only in the time of need? If you answered he is your go to only in the time of need then you need to re-evaluate your relationship with Jesus. He should be your first and your last all the time, not just your sometime. Be blessed.

Just a quick thought for today...

- -

Be an encourager

Lord I ask that you help me to always speak words of encouragement to everyone I come in contact with. Always lifting them up and letting them know how important they are to me. Allow me to be the woman described in Proverbs 31. Guide my every step and help me to always listen to your voice. Lord help me to live my life as an example for you so others may come to know you as their personal Lord and savior. Help me not to be a stumbling block but to be a helper to others as we travel this road called life. I pray that my brothers and sister have a blessed and prosperous life filled with love, joy and peace in Jesus name.

Be blessed.